LIVING COLOUR

BY LOUISE UPSHALL

GUMNUT MAGIC

Published in 2024 by Gumnut Magic

www.gumnutmagic.com

Credits
Page 78: Photograph by Stephanie Simcox, www.stephaniesimcoxphotography.com

ISBN 978-0-6459240-2-2

Acknowledgment of Country

This magazine was created while living and working on the Ngurra (Country) of the Darug and Gundungurra people, in what is now called the Blue Mountains, Australia.

I pay my respects to Darug and Gundungurra elders and ancestors, and to all the generations who have lived in and on and as part of Country. I honour their survival, their ongoing relationship with Country and their plant and colour knowledge and traditions.

Always was, always will be, Aboriginal land.

13

CONTENTS

31

19

51

59

67

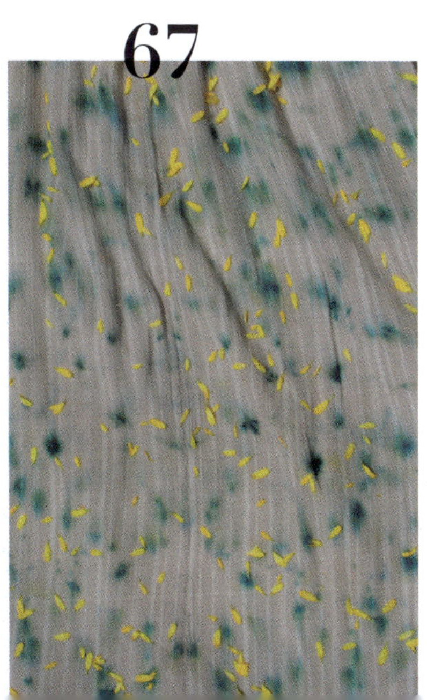

APPENDIX

LIVING COLOUR // Issue 1

It is a joy to welcome you to the first issue of *Living Colour*, a collection of projects and inspiration. Join me as we eco-print, eco-dye, sew and paint, craft and create with natural colours from the plants around us.

The tutorials in *Living Colour* will mainly cover natural dyeing techniques, including eco-printing. But we will make forays into other crafts and activities from time to time, and enjoy overlaps too - perhaps sewing a garment and then dyeing it, perhaps using the same plant to make both an ink and a dye.

My hope is that this magazine can be like a workshop that you can hold in your hands. It's not always possible to meet in person, and we already spend so much of our lives online. May these projects of living colour root you deeply in place, connecting with the plants around you and wearing the colours of nature.

In this issue there is a special focus on Black Knight scabiosa flowers. We will wander through my garden to pick some, then print and dye with them in a few different ways. If you're not currently growing any Black Knight scabiosa, there are suggestions for how to do these tutorials with other dyestuff instead. But if you love plants and natural dyeing, I really encourage you to grow this flower. Their intricate purple flowers brighten up the garden, and are beloved by butterflies, bees and other pollinators. They also look great in a home picked bouquet and when the flowers start to get a little old there are so many different uses for them, as you will see.

- Louise

Before you begin

The tutorials in *Living Colour* mostly focus on eco-printing and natural dyeing. Whether you are an adventurous beginner to these craft forms, an old hand, or somewhere in-between, you are welcome here.

Depending on your level of experience and your personality, you might like to follow my instructions exactly, down to the choice of dyestuff. Or you may prefer to treat the instructions simply as inspiration for your own experiments and wanderings.

Beginners will find the appendix useful, with its notes on fabric preparation, iron mordant and soy milk binder. If you are wanting a more solid introduction to eco-printing and/or natural dyeing, then I recommend my book, *Leaf & Colour*.

The instructions for many of the projects are based on preparing your fabric with soy milk binder. But if you are confident with other techniques such as mordanting with alum, then you can absolutely substitute those instead. Using different mordants, fabrics or dyestuff will of course affect the results you get, but maybe you delight in the mystery.

Whichever approach you take, I wish you so much joy and fulfillment in your journey.

Introduction to Black Knight scabiosa

Let's wander through the garden, getting to know this special dye plant. Where does it grow, how do we identify it, and why is it so special?

Growing notes

Black Knight scabiosa is a cultivar of *Scabiosa atropurpurea*. It is an ornamental plant that produces dark purple flowers covered in delicately shaped petals. The spiky seed heads are also striking, as shown overleaf.

Black Knight scabiosa is easy to grow from seed. Best planted in full sun positions, the plants can withstand a wide range of growing zones. In mild climates they are a short-lived perennial, but they don't do well with extreme heat or cold.

In cooler climates, plant them after the last frost for flowers in summer. They can survive light frosts, so you can also plant them in autumn and overwinter the young plants. This helps them to flower a bit earlier. Or plant them in both spring and autumn to get an extended flowering season. Because they are sensitive to extreme heat, if you live somewhere sub-tropical or tropical, you'll want to grow them over the winter.

Dye notes

I learnt about this remarkable dye plant via Liz Spencer (*The Dogwood Dyer*) and Rebecca Desnos, who in turn credit Kristin Morrison from *Love All Species*.

There are two special things about dyeing with Black Knight scabiosa. One is that their flowers create blue and purple dye, colours that are uncommon in the natural dye world. The petals contain such vivid colour that it starts to seep out as soon as the boiling water is poured on top. They are surprisingly potent so even a handful of flowers is enough to dye several small pieces of fabric.

The other special thing about these flowers in that the dye is pH sensitive. This means they can easily be modified to create greens and pinks as well, as we will do in the first project of this magazine.

A word of warning

But lest you think that this is the perfect dyestuff, please note that it is fugitive, and the colours will fade over time. Black Knight scabiosa is an anthocyanin dye, which is why its colours are pH sensitive and why it is fugitive.

Anthocyanin dyes are light sensitive, so are best used for dyeing items that will have minimal sun exposure. Black Knight scabiosa does have more lasting colour than some anthocyanin dyes, but it will still fade noticeably over time. Using it with an iron mordant, as we will do in a few of the projects, will extend the life of the colours. Or you can embrace the fleeting nature of the colour, and re-dye your items every year, to celebrate the annual scabiosa flowering.

Although fugitive colours have drawbacks, the colours are so special that I think it is worth accepting the fugitive nature of this dye plant. And once you try it, I'm sure you'll agree.

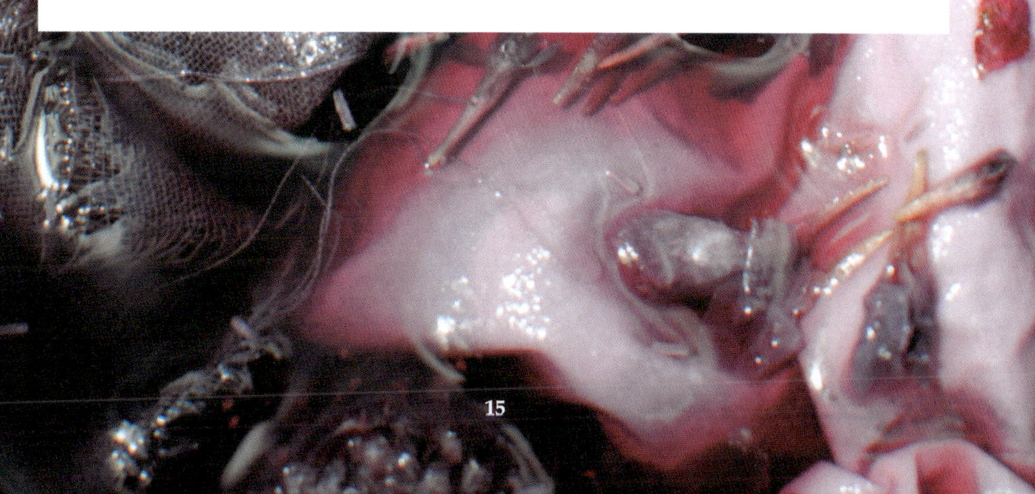

Flowers, leaves and seed heads

Black Knight scabiosa flowers are made up of abundant florets - miniature flowers clustered onto the flower head. These can be individually pulled off to eco-print or hammer into fabric. For simplicity's sake, I will refer to these florets as petals.

Black Knight scabiosa leaves come in an intriguing variety of shapes, which makes them fun to eco-print with. They also work well for the flower hammering technique.

The puffy, spiky seed heads lend them the common name pincushion flower, and can add interest to a dried bouquet.

Scabiosa dye patterns

Create gorgeous blue and purple fabric in a Black Knight scabiosa dye bath. Then use the magic of modifiers to paint bright pink, blue and green patterns on top!

When creating a dye bath with Black Knight scabiosa flowers, it is crucial not to boil it. Anthocyanin dyes are heat sensitive, so are easily damaged by overcooking.

Additionally, I have found that keeping the temperature very gentle, below a simmer, means that the dyed fabric will have quite dramatic colour shifts from the modifiers. If the dye is overcooked, you still get the blue-purple shades on the dried cloth but the colours won't shift as much when you use the modifiers.

Cotton prepared with soy milk binder and then dyed with these flowers will often look pink or purple in the dye bath, and then dry to a purple or blue colour, or a shade in between. Differences in cooking temperature and length of cooking can affect the exact shade you get.

Dyeing fabric

Step one: Gather some scabiosa flower heads. Put them in a pot and cover with boiling water. Heat gently for 15 minutes, keeping the temperature under a simmer. Let the dye bath sit for a few hours or overnight, and then repeat this process.

Step two: Add some pre-wetted fabric and heat gently for another 15 minutes. I used cotton prepared with soy milk binder. You can leave the flowers in the pot or strain them out. For maximum colour, let the fabric sit in the dye bath for a few hours and then reheat.

Step three: Once you are happy with the depth of colour of the fabric, remove it and rinse in plain water. Leave it to dry somewhere shady as the dye is very light sensitive.

Modifying colours

Once you have dyed some fabric, you can play with modifiers. I've painted patterns on the fabric with them, but you can also soak the whole cloth in a modifier to get a uniform colour change.

To use the modifiers, dissolve any powders in water, and dilute liquid modifiers with water too.

Alkaline modifiers

Alkalis can be used to shift colours towards blue and green. Alkaline modifiers include washing soda, baking soda, soda ash or wood ash water. To make the latter, collect wood ashes from a fireplace and soak them in a bucket of water for a week. Gently pour the top water out without disturbing the wood ash sediment that has settled to the bottom.

Acid modifiers

Acids can be used to shift the Black Knight scabiosa results towards pink and purple. Acidic modifiers include white vinegar (cleaning vinegar), lemon juice or citric acid.

Iron mordant

Homemade iron mordant can also be used as a modifier. It will darken the results to create dark blues and greens. It will also increase the colour fastness of the dye. You can find instructions for homemade iron mordant in the appendix.

Painting patterns

Top: Lines painted with vinegar to produce pink stripes on a purple background.

Middle: Painting spots with vinegar and dissolved washing soda. In some sections I have played around with painting one modifier, and then putting a drop of the other on top. Pushing the colour in one direction and then the other brings out slightly different shades than just using a single modifier.

Bottom: These spots were painted with dissolved washing soda (green) and diluted iron mordant (blue).

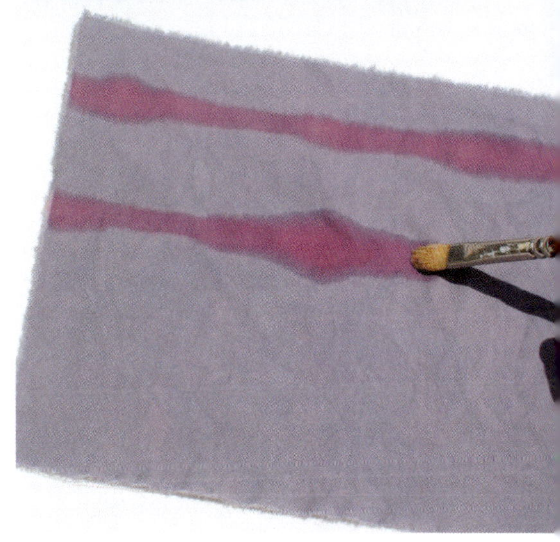

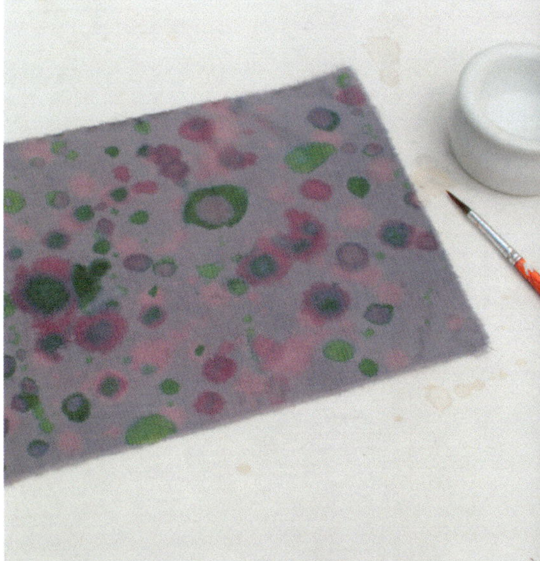

Scabiosa dye blanket on paper

Add simple but beautiful coloured backgrounds around your eco-prints, with the use of a dye blanket.

A dye blanket is a piece of fabric soaked in strong dye, that is placed over the leaves before you wrap up your bundle. Dye blankets are often used in fabric bundles, but here we are using them on paper. As the bundle cooks, the dye transfers onto the fabric or paper that it is in contact with, creating a solid colour around the eco-prints.

Creating a dye blanket

To create a dye blanket, start by making an extra strong dye bath. You can follow the instructions in the scabiosa dye patterns tutorial. But use as much dyestuff and as little water as possible, so that the dye is very strong. Then soak a piece of plain cotton in this dye. The cotton should be unmordanted and not prepared with soy milk binder either. We don't want the dye to bond to the blanket, we just want the blanket to hold the dye temporarily.

Dyestuff options

I've eco-printed with Japanese maple leaves here, but you can try any other eco-print leaves, such as eucalyptus, oak, strawberry or rose. And you can also make a dye blanket from any dye bath - onion skin, avocado, or your favourite flowers, leaves or bark are a good place to start. Ideally the colour of the dye blanket and the colour of the eco-print will be different, so that there is contrast between the print and the background.

Paper options

You can also try any kind of paper. I love using watercolour paper because it has a beautiful texture. Some artist quality watercolour paper is primed with gelatin. The proteins in the gelatin take up the dye really well, resulting in strong and bright colours. You can also experiment with any scrap paper from around your house, such as drawing paper, magazine pages, food packaging or old letters. Sometimes the prints on these can be just as good as on the expensive paper!

Scabiosa dye blankets on paper

Step one: Soak some leaves or flowers in iron mordant for a few minutes, then place them on pre-wetted watercolour paper. I'm using Japanese maple leaves, which I've placed with the back of the leaf facing down as this side generally gives more colour.

Step two: Cover the leaves with the dye blanket. This one was cut to size, but it can also be interesting to use a dye blanket that is smaller than the piece of paper, so that only some of the paper gets dye transferred onto it.

Step three: Press the paper and dye blanket between 2 tiles. Secure the tiles firmly with string, then simmer in plain water for about 30 minutes.

Results & variations

Top: This print was done on student quality watercolour paper. This absorbs the colour well and has a nice texture, but is cheaper than artist quality watercolour paper.

Middle and opposite: Here I've used Arches cold pressed watercolour paper. The gelatin this paper is primed with has absorbed the colour more strongly. Interestingly, this paper has produced more of a green result rather than the blue above.

Bottom: Here I re-used a piece of paper that had already been eco-printed with a few tests of different flowers and leaves, including scabiosa petals in the top left corner. Using a dye blanket is a good way to improve any uninspiring or pale eco-print results.

Hammered scabiosa petal prints

There are two different ways to get prints from scabiosa flower petals. Here we will hammer the petals and in the next tutorial we will eco-print with them instead.

There are advantages and downsides to both methods, so it comes down to which results you prefer the look of. Hammering the petals is a faster process, the prints are clearer, and you get a rich purple colour. The downside is that they are less colour fast than the eco-printed results.

You can also use this method with a range of other soft leaves and flowers. Some common garden plants that work well include the leaves of sage, maple, marigold, yarrow, purple basil, geranium, smoke bush and nasturtium. And flowers to try include wild pansy, violent, marigold, cosmos, coreopsis and nasturtium. Flat flowers can be used whole, while bulky flowers like the scabiosa work best if you just use the petals.

It's also beautiful to just wander around your garden or a local park, collecting one of each type of leaf and flower and trying it on a large piece of sample fabric. You will end up with a memento of the season, plus a visual reference for future hammering adventures.

For this tutorial I used fabric prepared with soy milk binder. I've since done lightfastness tests and found that preparing the fabric with iron mordant instead creates longer lasting prints. But it also shifts the colour of the scabiosa results to blue. If you are after purple, use soy milk binder which still has an adequate colour fastness.

Scabiosa hammered prints

Step one: Use a piece of clothing prepared with soy milk binder or iron mordant. Turn it inside out. This will allow you to print both the back and front at once. Place a piece of cardboard underneath the clothing, and on top of a hard surface such as a cement floor.

Step two: Put a scabiosa petal inside the garment and fold the fabric back over it.

Step three: Gently hammer the petal through the fabric. A small amount of colour will bleed through to the wrong side of the garment.

Step four: Carefully peel the fabric back to check that the petal has printed completely. If not, you can fold it back down and keep hammering.

Step five: Put more petals inside the garment and continue hammering until you are happy with the design.

Step six: Once your garment is complete, turn it right side out. Let it dry overnight, then carefully peel off any dried petals that are still stuck to it. Iron the garment on a low temperature to help set the colour. After wearing, wash gently by hand.

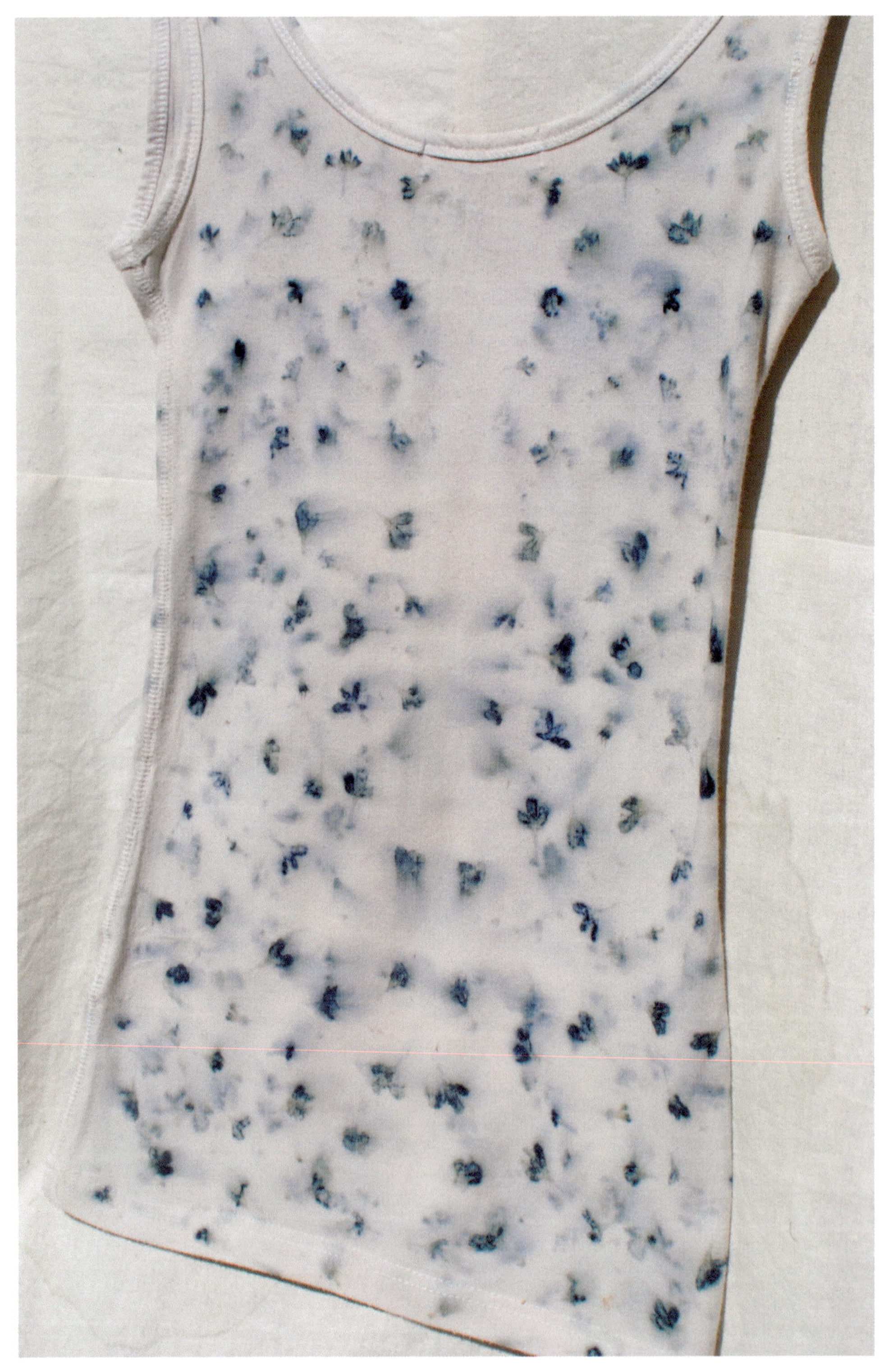

Scabiosa flower eco-prints on cotton and paper

Try eco-printing with scabiosa flowers to create dreamy, soft petal prints in shades of blue.

If you want to try eco-printing with your scabiosa petals instead, one advantage is that the prints are a bit more colour fast than the hammered results. Another benefit is that you can use dried flowers, which means you can still do this project after your plants have stopped flowering for the year. A downside to this method is that there is more colour bleeding than with the precise method of hammering the petals. But you might prefer the soft, watercolour effect.

Drying the flowers

To dry the scabiosa petals, carefully separate them out of the flower heads, lay them in a single layer on a piece of cardboard, cover with another piece of cardboard and then weigh down with books. Leave the petals until fully dry, and then store them in a small box or paper bag. The colour will eventually lessen so it is best to use them within a few months.

Preparing your fabric

I prepared this cotton top using iron mordant alone, although you could do a combination of soy milk binder and iron mordant for extra colour fastness. The iron helps the colour last longer, but remember that scabiosa is still a fugitive dye. Use it on garments that you aren't going to wear outside for long periods of time, and be prepared to re-print it over time.

Some other dyestuff to try

Some other flowers that you could try with this method include: Hollyhock (*Alcea rosea*), dyer's chamomile (*Anthemis tinctoria*), Marigold (*Tagetes* spp. including *Tagetes lucida*), dyer's coreopsis (*Coreopsis tinctoria*), and *Cosmos* spp. (including *Cosmos sulphureus*, *Cosmos bipinnatus*).

You can also use this same method with onion skins or with leaves such as eucalyptus, oak or Japanese maple. Use them as is, or try cutting or tearing them into little pieces for a completely different look! Onion skins work great for this.

Scabiosa eco-prints on cotton

Preparing your fabric: Pour a splash of iron mordant into a bucket of water. Wearing gloves, submerge a cotton top for a few minutes, then squeeze the excess water out and hang to dry in the shade.

Step one: Pre-wet your top. This is an important step because we are going to steam this bundle instead of simmering it in water. The water will help the colour transfer from petal to cotton. Arrange dried, pressed petals over half of the top.

Step two: Fold the other half on top and then cover half with petals again.

Step three: Fold the fabric in half again, then cover half with petals a final time.

Step four: After folding your fabric in half again, you'll now have a small stacked bundle. Cover the top and bottom in petals, and wrap in plain cotton to hold these final petals in place.

Step five: Press the cotton bundle between two tiles and tie tightly with string. Steam this bundle above boiling water for about half an hour. You could also submerge the bundle in water and simmer it instead, but this will cause more bleeding of colour than the steaming method.

Step six: After cooking, unwrap and wash the top immediately in warm water with a mild detergent. This will lessen the bleeding of colour, resulting in clearer prints when it dries.

Scabiosa eco-prints on paper

You can also eco-print with scabiosa flower petals on paper. The petals will leave prints on most types of paper, although the depth and clarity of the results will vary. The samples opposite were done on copy paper, a magazine page, student quality watercolour paper and Arches watercolour paper (from top to bottom).

Creating a paper bundle

To try it out, sprinkle scabiosa petals over some small pieces of paper. You may like to include other dyestuff too - at the start of the appendix is an example of paper eco-printed with scabiosa petals and iron-soaked dyer's chamomile leaves.

There are a few different ways that you can wrap your bundle. You can layer the paper between tiles as we did in the dye blanket tutorial. Or you can roll the paper around a rusty can. Either way, tie the bundle tightly with string.

Cooking your bundle

Cook your paper bundle for about half an hour. You can either steam or boil it. I've had very similar results from both methods. The advantage of boiling is that it's a bit simpler, and also gives you the option of cooking the bundle in a dye bath instead of water for some extra colour. If you prefer to steam your paper bundles, make sure that you wet the paper before wrapping it up, to help the colour transfer.

side the box
Mackintosh shares how handm
ity to create thoughtful keepsakes for your loved o
g thought into a gift for that special someone one
hard to top plan and let those creative juices flow
sy world. Often, it can be all too tempting to sh out
ething, however, it is possible to make the time to
As the s
You don't
somebody
baking, a p

Naturally dyed moons

After that deep dive into techniques using Black Knight scabiosa flowers, now let's move onto some other projects. First up is a method of resist dyeing. Resist dyeing involves covering a section of fabric to prevent dye from reaching it, creating a pattern of dyed and undyed sections. Many different materials can be used to make a resist, such as wax, paste, string, clamps or wooden shapes. Indonesian batik and ikat, Japanese shibori and Yoruba adire are some traditional practices of resist dyeing.

Moons are a simple resist dyeing project, where we use a circle to create the moons and then dye a sky colour around them. You can use any dark dye bath for this, such as black, grey or dark brown. I love using eucalyptus bark and iron for a smokey grey. But you can use your own favourite dark dyes - try adding a splash of iron mordant to acorns, black tea, black walnut husks or avocado dye baths. As shown in the variations, you can also dye the moons in an indigo vat to create a beautiful blue sky instead

Making mini moons

Step one: Gather a strip of prepared cotton, 2 circular relief shapes (I'm using Australian 20 cent coins) and clips or pegs for fastening the bundle.

Step two: Fold the fabric into a concertina fold. This will help each layer be more exposed to the dye bath. Here I am creating 3 layers of moons, which is a good number to start with. Any more than that and sometimes the edges of the moons start to get too blurry.

Step three: Place the circles in the centre of the folded fabric, on the front and back. Make sure they are lined up carefully with each other.

Step four: Hold the circles in place with pegs or clips. Try to only press the circles and not the fabric, or you will end up with relief marks around the moons.

Step five: Cook in a dark dye bath for about 1 hour and then remove immediately. If you let them sit in the dye bath, the dye may seep in, causing blurry edges.

Step six: Unwrap the bundle and enjoy the mini moons you have created.

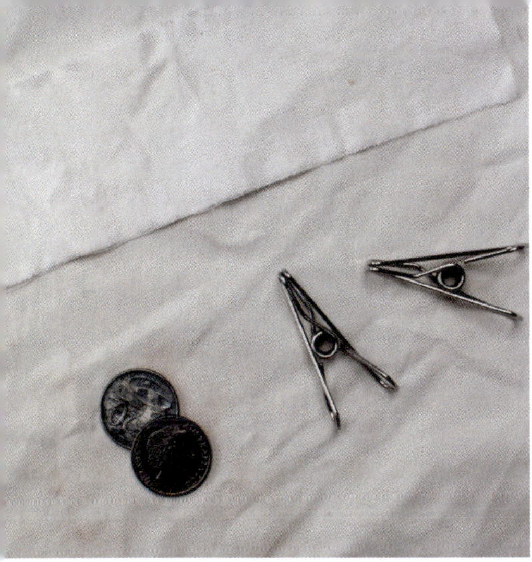

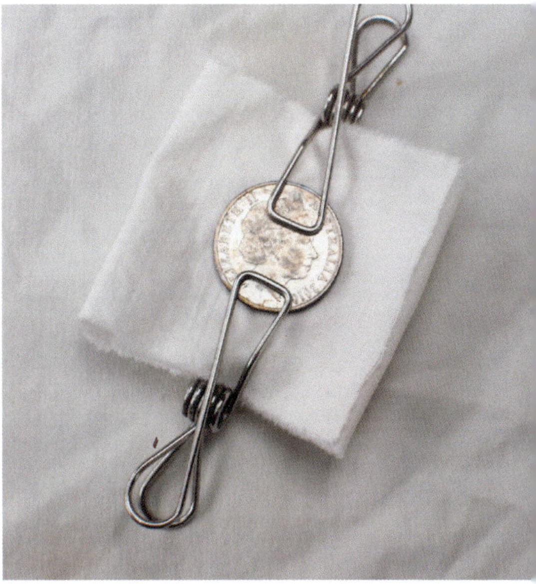

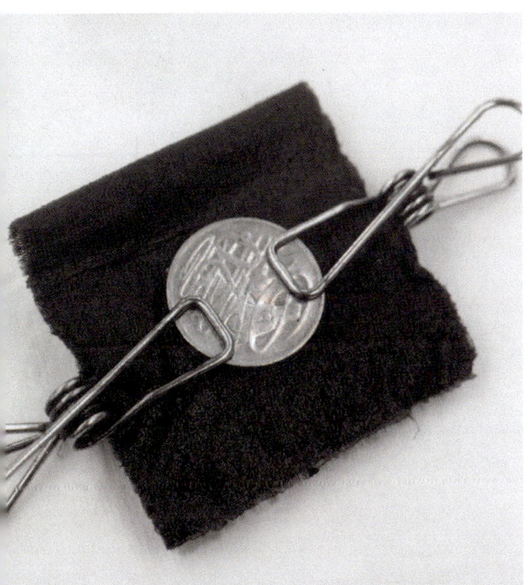

Large moons variations

Coins are a really easy starting point for your relief shapes, and create cute mini moons. But perhaps you would like to create larger moons. You can search second hand stores for flat metal circles to repurpose. I've collected some metal coasters that are great for making larger moons.

Another variation to try is instead of white fabric, using lightly eco-printed fabric that has subtle colour and shapes on it. This can make for a more interesting and textured moon, as shown below.

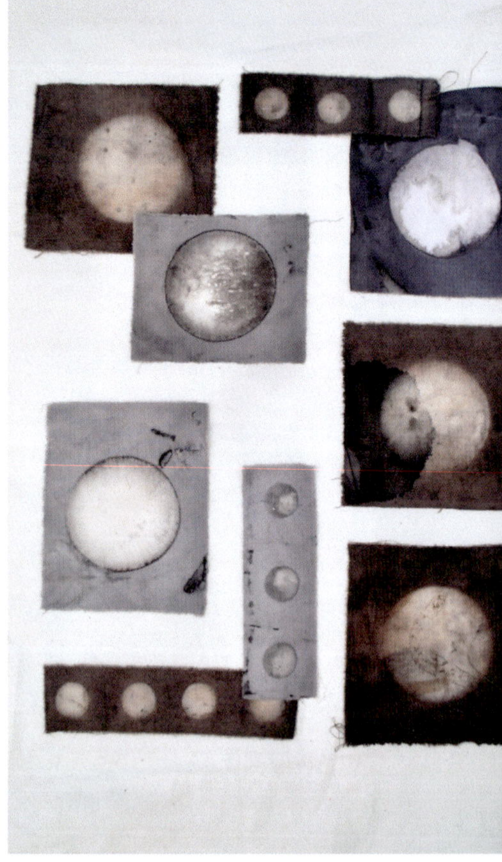

Colour variations

To create coloured moons, pre-dye your fabric before doing the resist dyeing. In the bottom left image, I used coreopsis flowers for the yellow moons and madder dye powder for the pink moons.

To create a blue sky around the moons, dye them in an indigo vat instead of a dye bath. In the bottom right image, you can see some moon samples made with indigo over white fabric and dyed fabric. There is also a half moon I created using half circle resist shapes cut out of sheets of copper.

Nettle ink

I've been drinking nettle infusions for years, and love their nourishing, energising powers. I've also been spilling nettle infusion on my kitchen bench for years and noticing what an intense green mark they leave. One day I decided to try them out as an ink. To start with, I simply put a few drops of the infusion onto paper. I was amazed by the vibrant greens they left behind, as shown opposite.

Over time, I experimented with different variables, such as using homegrown and store bought nettle, and soaking it for different lengths of time. Each time I make a new nettle ink, the colour is different - sometimes subtly so and sometimes more drastically. In this article I'll share which of the variables have produced the richest greens.

One of the special things about natural ink is that there are so many subtle shades. The different possible shades are influenced by many factors, including the origin and quality of the original dyestuff, the ratio of water to dyestuff, how long it was brewed for, whether you strained it, and how much ink you put on the paper. As with natural dyeing, there is not one right way to make ink, just different possible results.

In this article you'll see a few different shades of nettle green, and in your experiments you'll be able to discover more. What worked best for me might not work best for you. Instead of trying to replicate the shades I have gotten, I invite you to be curious about the process, to try different things, and to get to know the colours of the nettle that you have access to (whether that is plants from your garden or a local park, or dried nettle tea purchased from a store).

Nettle ink samples

Fresh nettle leaves: Soaked in boiling water overnight, then strained. So many subtleties emerged as this one dried - patches of yellow, green and blue.

Store bought dried nettle: Brewed for 3 hours. Not reduced. This method produced a medium green with a lovely dark ring around the edges. The sun reducing method described opposite could have helped create a darker green.

Dried nettle from my garden: Infused for two days, strained and then sun reduced to darken the colour. I was able to achieve the darkest and 'greenest' green by using dried, homegrown nettle and reducing the colour gently.

Making nettle ink

Nettle ink is made by covering dried nettle leaves in boiling water, then letting it soak for a day or longer. Use at least a handful of dried nettle. For the deepest colour, you want to use just enough water to cover the nettle. The reason that it is better to soak this ink rather than cooking it is that the green of nettle ink comes from chlorophyll, which is very heat sensitive. Cooking tends to turn the ink brown.

Once you are happy with the shade of green, strain it through fabric or a coffee filter. I've gotten the best greens by letting it brew for a few days, and then after straining letting it sit for another day or two. Sometimes the liquid will go brown when it is being made, but when left to sit it goes back to green.

If I want to get deeper shades, I'll leave the strained liquid in a small shallow bowl in direct sunlight. The heat will reduce the liquid and concentrate the green colour. This sun reduction method is gentler than trying to reduce the liquid through heating it on a cooktop, thus helping to retain the green colour, and it is also more suitable for reducing small amounts of dye.

After straining the ink, and reducing it if desired, your ink is ready. I use it on paper as is, but you could also experiment with binders such as gum arabic.

It can also be beautiful to use the nettle ink unstrained. Remove any visible pieces of nettle, but leave the very small particles in there. These will separate out and dry in an intriguing way, as shown in the top sample on the facing page. This effect is also visible in the photo at the start of this article.

You can also try combining several types of ink. The bottom two samples opposite are a combination of nettle ink and maple leaf ink. Make a circle of one ink and then carefully drop in small amounts of another ink, without mixing. As the ink dries, the colours will lightly mix and separate in interesting ways.

Now that you understand a few ways to make and use nettle ink, you may be wondering how colour fast it is. The green of the ink comes from chlorophyll which is a light sensitive pigment. So this ink may change colour eventually. But I've had some samples of nettle ink for over 3 years, stored away from direct sunlight, and the green is still looking good. If you wish to sell artworks made with nettle ink, you will need to do your own colour fastness tests. But if you are just playing with the ink, you can enjoy it as a living colour that may evolve over time, just as we do.

A safety note: For my nettle infusions and nettle ink, I use *Urtica dioica*, an edible plant known as stinging nettle or common nettle. Although it can cause an uncomfortable sting when you touch it, it is safe for our purposes here. Take care and do your own research if you are using other species of *Urtica*. Not all are safe to consume or touch. For example, the New Zealand species *Urtica ferox* has a toxic sting.

Resist shapes with eco-prints inside

When combining eco-printing and natural dyeing techniques, there are three different options. You can dye the bundle before eco-printing it, dye it after eco-printing it, or dye it at the same time. Here we will dye it at the same time, by cooking our eco-print bundle in a dye bath. Using a tile as a resist shape creates a white border around the eco-print, surrounded by the solid background of the dyed section.

In the following pages you'll find instructions for two different variations of this technique. I hope that you will use these as a starting point for your own folding experiments. If you are dyeing something larger, you could either use larger tiles or do more folds.

As always, you can follow my instructions exactly or substitute in your own choice of leaves and/or dyestuff. Maple, rose, blackberry or eucalyptus leaves would all work well for the leaf prints. You might also arrange multiple leaves or a small branch of leaves in each fold rather than a single leaf. There are endless possibilities for different combinations of leaves, dye baths and folding styles. Above all, have fun playing around!

A simple eco-print and resist shape combination

Step one: Place some iron-dipped leaves in the centre of your fabric. Here I have used a single geranium leaf on both the front and back of a small cotton singlet. The singlet was prepared with soy milk binder.

Step two: Place a tile over the leaves on the front and back of the fabric, carefully lining up the edges of both tiles to create a sandwich.

Step three: Hold the tiles in place with clamps, string or rubber bands. Clamps allow you to press the tiles without pressing the fabric, but using string will create some interesting relief marks around the tiles, so you may want to play with both options.

Step four: Simmer the bundle in a dye bath for about 1 hour. I used onion skins and put them in at the same time as the bundle, but you can also create a dye bath first. I also added a splash of iron mordant to darken the dye bath, but this is optional.

Step five: Leave the fabric in the dye bath until cool, so it can pick up the maximum amount of dye. In this example, the onion skins have created a solid olive green dye around the tiles.

Step six: Remove the tiles to reveal the relief shape that have been created, as well as the leaf prints.

Resist shape variation

This variation involves folding the garment into a concertina fold with leaves pressed between each layer.

Step one: Place an iron-dipped leaf (or several leaves) in the middle third of the garment.

Step two: Fold the top third of fabric down over the middle third.

Step three: Turn the top over and place another leaf on the middle third of this side.

Step four: Fold the bottom third of the fabric up over the middle third. Place a final leaf on both the top and bottom of the folded fabric.

Step five: Press the leaves and fabric between two tiles. I've placed mine on an angle to create a diamond resist pattern, but they can also be placed straight on to create a square resist instead.

Step six: Hold the tiles together firmly with string, rubber bands or a clamp.

Step seven: Cook the bundle in a dye bath for 1 hour, to create a solid colour around the tiles. Let the bundle cool in the dye bath, then remove and unwrap.

Step eight: Once unwrapped, admire the multiple leaf prints and relief shapes that have been created.

Colour fields

Often when eco-printing we are trying to get distinct leaf or flower shapes. But it can also be beautiful to create what I like to call a colour field - patches of different colours created by sprinkling a range of small dyestuff all over a piece of fabric. Flower petals, teas and spices work well for this, and you can also tear leaves and onion skins into small pieces.

In the following pages I show the process of making two different colour fields. But you can use the same method to experiment with any dyestuff available to you. It's hard to go wrong because you're not aiming for distinct prints or specific outcomes. Choose 2-3 different dyestuff to try, preferably ones that dye different colours or at least different shades.

In the colour field tutorial, I demonstrate how to roll the bundles up in a wrapping cloth, to get the pattern all over. But an interesting variation to try is omitting the wrapping cloth and instead tying the rolled bundle up in string and cooking it in a dye bath. This will create solid sections of dye on the outside of the bundle, which will blend into the colour field inside the bundle.

Colour field project

Step one: Gather a small selection of dyestuff. In this example, I have used whole cloves, fresh coreopsis petals, rooibos tea and dried calendula petals. Some other simple dyestuff to try include turmeric, black tea and small pieces of brown onion skin.

Step two: Sprinkle the dyestuff over a garment or piece of fabric. You can sprinkle them evenly all over, or create stripes or patterns of different dyestuff.

Step three: If your garment has sleeves, fold them in one at a time, sprinkling more dyestuff on top of each sleeve as you go.

Step four: Roll up the garment or fabric. By rolling it up, the back of the garment will also come in contact with the sprinkled dyestuff. To create colour on the last bit of the bundle, sprinkle extra dyestuff onto a piece of plain fabric and roll the bundle onto this.

Step five: Keep rolling until the garment is fully enclosed by the wrapping cloth, and then fold both ends over. Tie the bundle tightly with string, simmer for 1 hour, then let it cool in the pot.

Step six: Unwrap the bundle and admire your colour field!

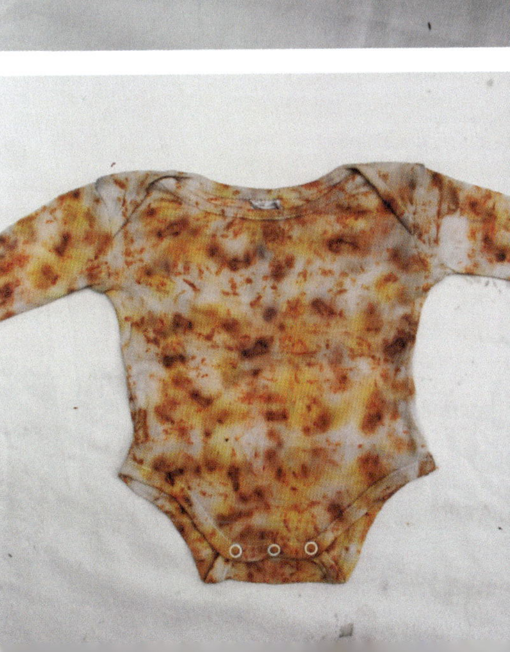

Scabiosa colour field

This viscose dress was prepared with soy milk binder, sprinkled with Black Knight scabiosa petals, rolled up and simmered for 30 minutes, to create the soft blue and green prints visible on this page. It was then sprinkled with dyer's chamomile petals, rolled up and simmered for another hour, to add patches of yellow. It's not necessary to do it in two stages, I was simply testing the scabiosa petals alone to begin with before deciding to create a more complex colour field.

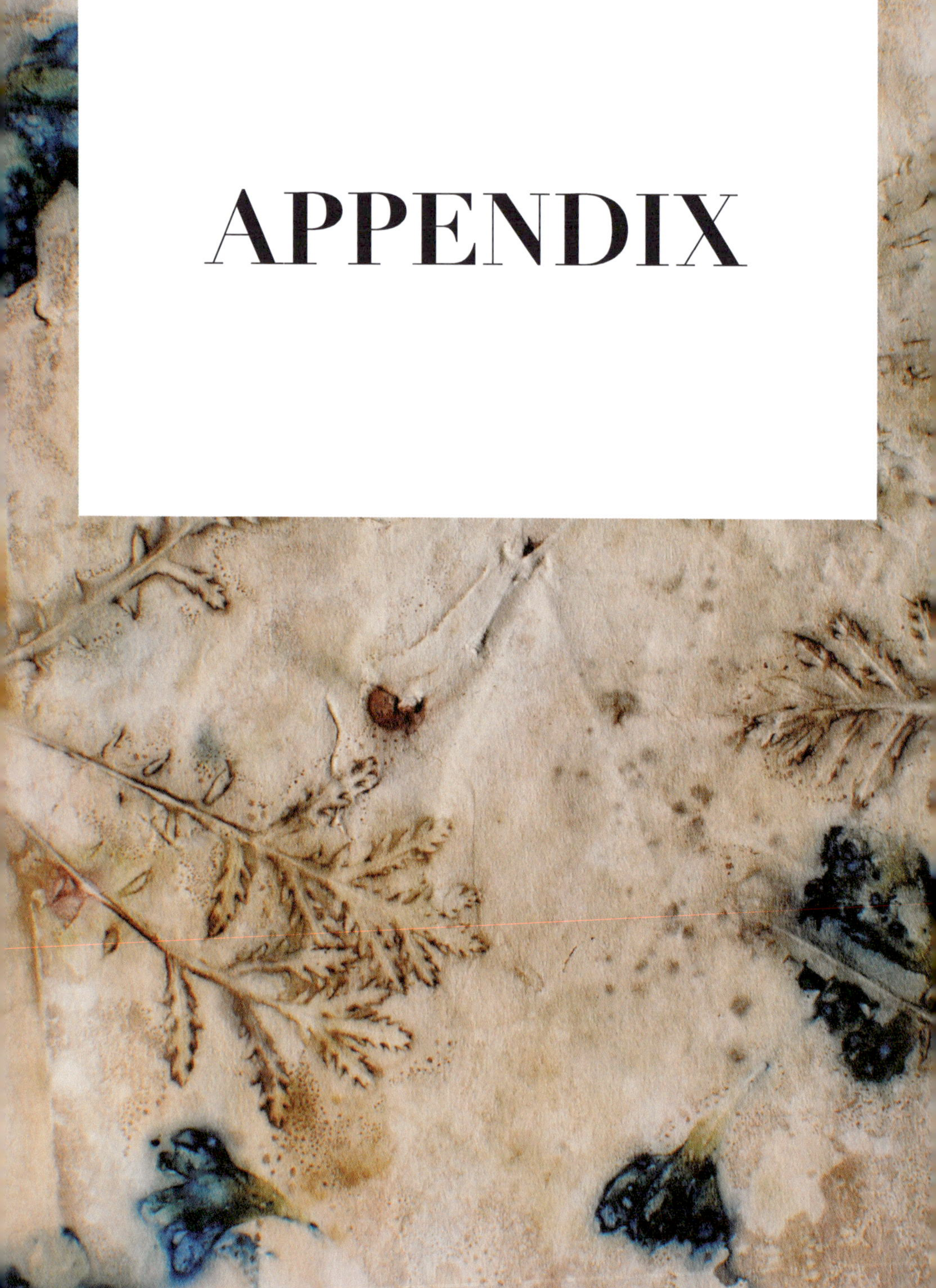

APPENDIX

Safety

• Wear gloves while handling iron mordant.

• Use dedicated equipment for dyeing with (dye pot, spoons etc.)

• Cook your bundles somewhere with good ventilation (outside if possible, or with an open window or exhaust fan)

• Avoid using plants which could cause hazardous fumes or skin irritation.

Pre-washing fabric

It is a good idea to wash your fabric before eco-printing or natural dyeing. New fabric is often coated in waxes, oils and pectic substances that will inhibit the take up of dye. The simplest method is to use old clothing or fabric that you know has been washed lots of time.

If you want to pre-wash cellulose (plant based) fabric, but still keep things simple, add them in when you are doing a hot machine wash. Use a mild detergent and if you are using new fabric or clothing, wash them several times.

For a more thorough pre-washing, you can scour your fabric. Scouring is a special type of deep washing used to prepare fabric for natural dyeing. Overleaf you will find recipes for scouring cellulose and protein fibres.

To scour, you will need a pH neutral scouring agent such as Synthrapol or Orvus Paste, or a neutral dishwashing liquid. For cellulose fabric, you will also need soda ash or washing soda. The amount you use is calculated as a percentage of the weight of fibre (w.o.f.). For example, if you are scouring 500 grams of cotton, adding scouring agent at 1% w.o.f. requires adding 5 grams.

Scouring cellulose (plant based) fibres

Step one: Weigh your fabric. Then put it in a large pot and cover with warm water. Make sure it can move freely to ensure even scouring.

Step two: Add soda ash at 2% w.o.f. **OR** washing soda at 4% w.o.f. **PLUS** scouring agent at 1% w.o.f. **OR** dishwashing liquid at 2% w.o.f.

Step three: Simmer for about 1 hour. Let the pot cool down and then rinse the fabric well in warm water.

Scouring protein fibres (wool or silk)

Step one: Weigh your fabric. Then put it in a large pot and cover with warm water. Make sure it can move freely to ensure even scouring.

Step two: Add scouring agent at 1% w.o.f. **OR** dishwashing liquid at 2% w.o.f.

Step three: Heat gently for about 1 hour. Make sure not to simmer the fabric or agitate it, as you don't want to damage the fabric or cause the wool to felt. Let the pot cool down and then rinse the fabric well.

Making and using iron mordant

Make your own iron mordant (ferrous acetate) by collecting some small pieces of rusty iron or steel. Put them in a jar and cover with white (cleaning) vinegar. As soon as the vinegar starts changing colour, you can begin using your mordant, but it will get stronger over time. Whenever you use your mordant, top it up with more vinegar. If you don't use it regularly, make sure you add more vinegar every couple of months. It needs to be kept acidic to work optimally.

There are two main ways of using the iron mordant. To mordant cotton, add a splash of iron mordant to a bucket of water. Add in some pre-wetted fabric, and let it soak for a few minutes. Then remove and dry in the shade. The other method is to soak fresh leaves in the mordant. After a few minutes of soaking, you can use them to eco-print on plain fabric or fabric prepared with soy milk binder.

Iron mordant can also be used as a post-modifier. After dyeing or eco-printing an item, soak it in some watered down mordant to shift or darken the colours. Go slowly with this - it is always possible to add more mordant, but not to remove an overzealous use of it.

Safety note: Make sure that you are using iron/steel (confirmed through the presence of reddish rust). If you aren't sure, don't use it. And wear gloves every time you handle the mordant, including when you touch wet mordanted fabric or iron-soaked leaves. There are likely to be small amounts of other metals in the mordant that would be better not to touch.

Making soy milk binder

Option 1: using soybeans

Step one: For every 100 grams of fabric, use around 40 grams of soybeans. Cover your soybeans with water and soak overnight.

Step two: Place soybeans in a blender with plenty of water. Blend until smooth. Strain this liquid through a cloth, squeezing to get as much out as possible.

Step three: Return the soybean mush to the blender and add more water. Blend and strain. Repeat this step a few times, combining all of the liquid together. Once you have exhausted the soybean mush, you can compost it or bury it in your garden.

Option 2: using soy milk

Dilute 1 litre of soy milk with approximately 5 litres of water. It should look slightly translucent but not too watery.

Using soy milk binder

Step one: Pour your soy milk into a bucket or pot. Pre-wet your fabric, then add it in. Let the fabric sit in the soy milk for about 12 hours, or overnight. Store it in a cool place. If it's a hot day you can use ice cubes to keep it cool (thank you to Phoebe Hunter from *HunterMade* for that brilliant tip!)

Step two: Remove your fabric, squeezing out as much soy milk as possible. You can put it on a spin cycle in the washing machine or simply squeeze it out by hand. Hang the fabric to dry.

Step three: Once your fabric is dry, re-submerge it briefly in the soy milk, just long enough for it to get saturated again. Squeeze the fabric out well and hang it to dry, then repeat this step one more time. If the soy milk gets smelly, stop soaking and discard the liquid immediately, or else you will end up with pungent fabric.

Step four: Let this fabric cure for at least a week before dyeing it. You can store the fabric for a few months before use, but try to use it within a year.

About the author

Louise is an artist, mother and eco-printer living in the Blue Mountains of Australia. Natural dyeing brings together her love of craft, sewing, plants, gardening and writing. Under the label *Gumnut Magic*, she produces a small range of naturally dyed clothing and fabric, and teaches workshops and online courses. She also writes books and ebooks. Find more at gumnutmagic.com or connect on Instagram (@gumnutmagic).

Want to dive deeper?

Learn more about eco-printing and natural dyeing with my book, *Leaf & Colour*. I'll guide you through each step of the process. With a focus on natural materials and simple methods, it is easy to get started or to deepen your existing dyeing practice.

Available at gumnutmagic.com

Printed in Great Britain
by Amazon

45009556R00048